BACKYARD WILDLIFE

Owls

by Kari Schuetz

BELLWETHER MEDIA · MINNEAPOLIS, MN

Note to Librarians, Teachers, and Parents:

Blastoff! Readers are carefully developed by literacy experts and combine standards-based content with developmentally appropriate text.

Level 1 provides the most support through repetition of high-frequency words, light text, predictable sentence patterns, and strong visual support.

Level 2 offers early readers a bit more challenge through varied simple sentences, increased text load, and less repetition of high-frequency words.

Level 3 advances early-fluent readers toward fluency through increased text and concept load, less reliance on visuals, longer sentences, and more literary language.

Level 4 builds reading stamina by providing more text per page, increased use of punctuation, greater variation in sentence patterns, and increasingly challenging vocabulary.

Level 5 encourages children to move from "learning to read" to "reading to learn" by providing even more text, varied writing styles, and less familiar topics.

Whichever book is right for your reader, Blastoff! Readers are the perfect books to build confidence and encourage a love of reading that will last a lifetime!

This edition first published in 2012 by Bellwether Media, Inc.

Library of Congress Cataloging-in-Publication Data
Schuetz, Kari.
 Owls / by Kari Schuetz.
   p. cm. – (Blastoff! Readers : Backyard wildlife)
 Includes bibliographical references and index.
 Summary: "Developed by literacy experts for students in kindergarten through grade three, this book introduces owls to young readers through leveled text and related photos"–Provided by publisher.
 ISBN 978-1-60014-598-8 (hardcover : alk. paper)
 1. Owls–Juvenile literature. I. Title.
 QL696.S8S38 2012
 598.9'7–dc22   2011002253

Printed in the United States of America, North Mankato, MN.

080111   1187

Contents

Owls are **raptors** with flat faces and hooked **beaks**. They have large eyes.

Owls cannot
move their eyes.
They must turn
their heads to
look around.

Owls hear better than any other kind of bird. They hear up to ten times better than people!

Owls live in grasslands, forests, and **tundras**. Many **nest** in trees or barns.

Most owls hunt from a **perch**. They wait for mice, birds, and other **prey** to come near.

Owls then swoop down silently. They use their sharp **talons** to grab prey.

talons

Owls swallow prey whole or tear it apart with their beaks.

Owls cannot **digest** all parts of their prey. They spit out **pellets** of bones and hair.

Owls use sounds to talk to each other. Many hoot or screech. Hooooo! Hooooo!

Glossary

beaks—the mouths of some animals such as birds and turtles

digest—to break down into pieces

nest—to make a home

pellets—objects owls spit out; pellets include bones, hair, and other parts of prey owls cannot digest.

perch—a tree branch or other high place where a bird sits

prey—animals that are hunted by other animals for food

raptors—birds that are skilled hunters; raptors use sharp eyesight, great hearing, and sharp talons to hunt prey.

talons—sharp claws on the toes of some birds; all raptors have talons.

tundras—large, flat areas of frozen land without trees

To Learn More

AT THE LIBRARY

Gibbons, Gail. *Owls*. New York, N.Y.:
Holiday House, 2005.

Markle, Sandra. *Owls*. Minneapolis, Minn.:
Carolrhoda Books, 2004.

Mason, Adrienne. *Owls*. Tonawanda, N.Y.:
Kids Can Press, 2004.

ON THE WEB

Learning more about
owls is as easy as 1, 2, 3.

1. Go to www.factsurfer.com.

2. Enter "owls" into the search box.

3. Click the "Surf" button and you will see a
   list of related Web sites.

With factsurfer.com, finding more information
is just a click away.

Index

The images in this book are reproduced through the courtesy of: David Davis, front cover, p. 5; Juan Martinez, pp. 7, 13 (right); Amber Barger/Photolibrary, p. 9; Ronnie Howard, p. 11; Lakov Kalinin, p. 11 (left); Andrey Tiyk, p. 11 (middle); Jeffrey T. Kreulen, p. 11 (right); Robert Franz/KimballStock, p. 13; Anna Kravchuk, p. 13 (left); John A. Anderson, p. 13 (middle); Cusp and Flirt/Masterfile, p. 15; Visuals Unlimited/Masterfile, p. 17; Adri Hoogendijk/Minden Pictures, p. 19; Walter G Arce, p. 21.